THE PLAYFUL POWER OF METAPHOR:
Harness the Winds of Creativity, Innovation and Possibility

By Christie Latona and Janet Fox

Editor: Martha Murphy
Graphic Design and Illustrations: David Plihal

To order more copies of this book, please contact:
Fun & Done Press
PO Box 10951
Silver Spring, MD 20914
800.507.2959 or online at:
www.playfulpower.com

Please call us about our bulk-discount rates.
We seek to make distribution of the ideas
contained within this book widely accessible to
help organizations of all sizes create
cultures of creative thinking and innovation.

TABLE OF CONTENTS

PREFACE

Chances are you're living with unnecessary suffering, struggle, strife and stress. You have big ugly tasks weighing you down and big beautiful dreams that you can't get started on. You have tedious projects and promising initiatives that you can't seem to wrap up. You may have relationships that feel hopelessly stuck, ambitions that have landed in the ditch and plans that aren't going anywhere.

The frustrating part is that you usually know what you need to do to get things moving. Most of the time, you don't need more know-how or a new set of skills. Another diet book, another video on leadership, another manual on clutter control, another pep talk on the benefits of the proposed change are probably not going to get you up and running.

And you probably already have a sense of what success will look like. Whether it's getting the organization restructured or getting the garage cleaned out, launching the new product or learning Spanish, you've got a clear enough idea of where you want to end up and what it will take to get you there.

But between awareness and action, between the plan and the pay-off, there is a gap. For some reason, or for many reasons, you can't always get yourself to do what you know you want to do, or must do.

We encourage you to use this book to access and accomplish more of what you dream of by enlisting the playful power of metaphor and analogy. Scattered throughout the book are stories, exercises and examples that serve to embed the concepts presented in the text in different ways.

In our experience working with corporations, institutions, groups and individuals — whatever our title or official role — we both tend to be creative change agents, coaches and facilitators of personal growth and organizational development. This book grew out of what we have learned from all the seriously playful work we do. We dedicate it to advancing the abundance of playful power in your life.

Christie Latona & Janet Fox
October 2005

QUEſTIONſ ARE LIKE ſCALPELſ, METAPHORſ LIKE ſAILſ.

As we listen to the stories that people tell us about their life and situations, we are often struck by how "scripted" some stories become. You know, the story about how a sister was more popular, about how mean the kids at school were, about how being a large man with a loud voice or a petite blonde woman with a soft voice led people to jump to false assumptions and stereotypes.

An important part of exploring what is possible is freeing ourselves from the limiting scripts we carry with us and then improvising with our whole being. One of the best ways of actually accomplishing this is through using metaphor, analogy and other artistic, nonlinear techniques. Bringing metaphor to our attempts to change helps ensure that we don't just swap one script for another. Sometimes we must engage the mind's eye (not the mind's mouth) to help us "see" things in a more productive light.

Paintings, films, drama, dance, poems, photos and songs tell us things that words alone could never tell us. In fact, the cliché that "a picture is worth a thousand words" is an understatement. Words don't begin to express all that an artistically painted, filmed or photographed image does.

In our view, self-improvement programs that don't incorporate imagery or another artistic medium end up being less powerful and engaging experiences than those that are soaked in metaphor. We have seen that changes in atti-

"The metaphor is perhaps one of man's most fruitful potentialities. Its efficacy verges on magic, and it seems a tool for creation which God forgot inside one of His creatures when He made him."

~ Jose Ortega y Gasset

tudes, beliefs and behaviors occur more easily when intuition, pattern-recognition, symbolization and other "right brain" attributes are brought to bear on the challenge. An allegorical approach elicits these kinds of perceiving and knowing.

Metaphor and Other Figures of Speech

Metaphor originally stems from Greek words meaning "to bear or carry" and "a change." In language, a metaphor is defined as a direct comparison between two seemingly unrelated subjects. Typically, a first object is described as being or having the properties of a second object. In this way, the first object can be economically described because implicit and explicit attributes from the second object can be used to fill in the description of the first.

Relationship to other figures of speech

A **simile** is like a metaphor, in that both compare one object with another, but while a metaphor is implicit, a simile makes the comparison explicit with a word such as "like," "as," or "than." In this respect, a metaphor is a more concrete assertion of identity, and may result in confusion if taken literally, whereas a simile is clearly just a comparison.

Allegory is an extended section of prose or verse which carries a meaning or message about something other than its literal subject. Though it is similar to other rhetorical comparisons, an allegory is sustained longer and fuller in its details than a metaphor, and appeals to imagination where an analogy appeals to reason. The fable or parable is a short allegory with one definite moral.

Taken from: **http://en.wikipedia.org/wiki/Metaphor**

JELF-DIJCOVERY IJ LIKE...

Is your self-discovery process like drilling for oil or like catching the wind? Both approaches seek to convert a raw material into useable energy. Yet one uses a non-renewable resource, and the other a renewable one. One requires drilling into the earth; the other builds upon the earth. We always have a choice about how we approach any task or situation. There isn't one right approach, but one might be better than another based on how energized it make us feel.

Is your self-analysis process like dissecting a frog or like observing one? Let's say we want to be able to train humans to jump farther, and we have determined that frogs are the ideal benchmark. We could dissect a frog's leg and a human's leg to see how they differ, or we could watch the frog jump and watch the human jump and record the differences. When we dissect something, we discover the details of how that something works in a mechanistic fashion. When we observe non-judgmentally, we reveal something less precise, but more complex.

In situations where we want to understand why we behave in particular ways, and what it would take to make us change, asking questions is a tried-and-true way of eliciting information. Counselors and psychotherapists depend on questioning to arrive at a diagnosis as well as for a treatment tool. Consultants depend on questioning to conduct assessments. Coaches, trainers and good teachers of all kinds frequently employ a Socratic questioning approach to draw out answers.

But questioning alone may not be the best way to evoke breakthrough insights or to spur effective action. What often works more deeply and dramatically is a way of knowing that precedes questioning – both in human evolution and in the lives of every human being. And that way of knowing about the outer world and the inner world is by analogy, allegory and metaphor.

Little children, wise elders, poets and plumbers and programmers and politicians naturally use metaphor and analogy to communicate what they observe and how they feel:

My love is like a red, red rose.

—

You are the wind beneath my wings.

—

That cloud looks like a bear.

—

I can see clearly now, the rain has gone.

—

This is like herding cats.

—

Get ready to drink from a fire hose.

—

But here's the silver lining.

—

Busy as a beehive.

—

I feel like I have a target painted on my back.

—

Hungry as a wolf.

—

Climb every mountain, ford every stream,
follow every rainbow, till you find your dream.

And on, and on. We can only think rationally about things for which we have words. Yet many innovative and breakthrough ideas are pre-verbal — just out of our minds' reach — or beyond words. These inklings may come to us as visual images in our minds or as dream images. Or, we may recognize them and resonate with them in some actual object or event in the world. A painting or a piece of music, for example, may exactly correspond to some vague, unnamed internal knowledge.

Expressing ourselves by telling what something is like allows us more freedom and risk-taking than trying to provide a precise description of our situation and feelings. You can probably think of instances in which you or someone you were trying to help struggled to give a detailed account of exactly what was going on, only to continue to feel frustrated and stymied. Metaphors seem to help illuminate both problems and solutions partly because of their very lack of precision. Every place where the analogy breaks down becomes a space to be filled in from imagination and elaborated on in individual stories.

Allegories and metaphors work because they capture the essence of meaning without becoming trapped by particulars. Sometimes in order for us to understand something, a bit of its mystery must be preserved. Often we are best served by seeing the shape of the truth, without a lot of specificity. That may enable us to climb out of our rut without creating a new rut, or to step out of our script rather than exchanging it for another script.

For example, Martha may say that she feels like Cinderella in the way she is treated at work. She does all the dirty work and is always at the beck and call of arrogant, powerful people who don't appreciate her. She continues with this story line, adapting it to create her own version. She acknowledges that she is not waiting for a prince to sweep her away from the daily grind, but would love a fairy godmother. She then goes on to imagine and articulate what her fairy godmother might be and what kind of future would make her happy ever after. Instead of providing an absolute goal, it provides a direction for the evolution of a solution.

Or, Steven might describe himself as being like a football being tossed back and forth by two bosses he has to satisfy. In exploring that image, though, he notes that the football

3 Quick Ways to Add the Power of Metaphor to Your Life

1. **Extend intuitive inklings into a metaphor.** Open yourself up to getting information from all your senses — especially the mysteries of the sixth sense. When you speak of your situation, how does it feel? Describe your feelings using allegory or metaphor, and then ask yourself a perspective shifting "What" question.

   For example:
   - I feel as cold as ice. What would it take to thaw out?
   - I feel like a car spinning out of control. What would it take to prevent a wreck?
   - I feel like a swimmer struggling against the undertow in the ocean. What is the undertow? What is the shore?

2. **Create mini-role plays.**
   - Imagine you are a grand illusionist. What illusion would you like to create? What would you make appear or disappear? What do you have to practice to make it so?
   - You are a gardener surveying the flower beds around you. What is it time to do? What needs weeding, planting, watering, or pruning?

3. **Put context around a shift with as few words as possible.**
   - What would change about this situation if you viewed it as a journey instead of a destination?
   - Does this feel like a condemned building or a simple remodel?

doesn't feel anything, whereas he experiences stress and resentment. The very point at which the analogy breaks down — the football doesn't have any choice at all about whether or not it gets used — provides the opportunity for him to discover something: he probably does have some options that it's time to look at.

Mental images and metaphors are a powerful and time-honored way to tap into a vast store of inner wisdom. Throughout history, symbol systems have enabled people to connect with the attitudes and attributes that are available to them in times of any kind of need. The archetypes described by Carl Jung, the gods and goddesses of ancient Greece and Rome and the Tarot are a few such storehouses of universal truths about what it means to be human. In each case, the individual draws on a specific, yet essentially timeless, image to shed light on a particular situation in his or her own life.

Build Your Own Allegory

1. Think of a problem you are struggling with or a situation where you feel stuck or bored. Then fill in the blanks below using the first response that comes to mind.

2. Choose an animal _____ (A)

3. I feel like a (A) that is _____ (B)

4. I feel like a (A) that is (B). I wish I could _____ (C)

5. If I were a (A) that is (B) and wants to (C),
   I would _____ (D)

Read through the complete sentence in step 5. What ideas or images emerge when you compare these sentences to your problem?

For example, Georgia was struggling about asking her boss for a raise for some of her people. Her sentence #5 was: If I were a <u>turtle</u> that is <u>unappreciated</u> and wants to <u>be noticed</u>, I would <u>shed my shell</u>. That image enabled Georgia to shift her focus from worry about asking to a more productive imagining of the conversation she would have without her shell.

After you've done a few with animals as the noun in #2, you can branch out and fill in any noun of your choice. For example, Andre was feeling that he didn't have many friends and was perplexed about what to do. His sentence #5 was: If I were a <u>mall</u> that is <u>empty</u>, I would <u>sell better products</u>. That image told him in a quick and powerful way that he needed to change his attitude about and behaviors with people.

This tool is also available for free online at **www.playfulpower.com.**

WINDS OF CHANGE

Let's look at the whole issue of transforming awareness to action in terms of a windmill. The wind represents environmental trends, possibilities and energy available to us and the windmill represents us.

There are many elements of the windmill that make it more or less effective at capturing the power of the wind and converting it to something that serves its purpose. Some windmills grind corn, others chop wood, others generate electricity. Each useful outcome is a fulfillment of that windmill's purpose.

In the base of the windmill is the mechanism that controls which direction the sails face (choose). The sails (be) catch the wind and spin (do). At the apex of the arms of a windmill is the generator that converts mechanical energy into the purpose.

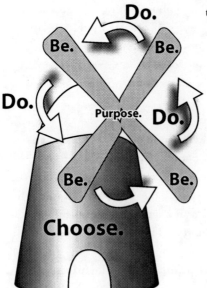

Imagine you are a windmill standing in the middle of an open, windy field. You have a choice about which direction to turn the sails to maximize contact with the wind. The sails represent the degree to which you are able to engage with the wind. If a sail is torn or damaged or distracted — even if it is in the right position to capture the wind — it will not spin. The choices we make about choosing our mindset are like the mechanism that controls the positioning of the sails.

Notice that without a clear focus or purpose, all of the spinning in the world doesn't yield anything of value; purpose is like the engine that converts mechanical energy to productive capacity. All of us can easily think of instances where we were frenzied, but not productive. That is the distinction between sails that are spinning and a windmill that is producing.

Choose is an opposite of just going through the motions and also an opposite of struggling to catch the wind. It may involve choosing your perspective, your environment, your companions and other things within your control. No matter how stuck we feel, there are always options. Sometimes we need to become aware of the many options available to us. In other instances, too many possibilities are the cause of our paralysis. We don't act because we literally don't know which way to turn. The choice has an impact on the quality of energy available to you.

Be is an opposite of understanding. Being is the bridge between knowing and doing. We use "be" as another word for "engagement." It means fully immersing yourself in the choice you have made. It means throwing yourself heart and soul into the approach you have decided on. It means listening to your gut and getting feedback from your environment so that adjustments are natural. This sail on the windmill directly impacts the intensity and amount of energy available for use.

Do changes reality and is created by the true engagement of Being. When you're fully engaged in a course you have chosen for yourself, "Doing" ceases to be a problem. "Doing" is the natural outcome and expression of "Being." This is the actual speed that the windmill spins and determines the resulting outcome in terms of fulfilling your purpose.

"Insight is like a cool breeze on a warm day. While it feels good, it may not help us do something differently or better."

~ Christie Latona

One obvious downfall of windmills as a power source is the fact that windmills don't have any control over the wind. Likewise, there are many things in our environment over which we have no control. The difference between windmills and human beings is that human beings have the means of generating wind in the form of passion.

During the remainder of this book, we will explore how to keep ourselves energized through the use of a metaphoric tool that facilitates the process of Choosing, Being and Doing. And, we will address many common windbreakers, including negative emotions, that prevent us from achieving our dreams.

Love It, Lose It or Choose It

You undoubtedly have many tasks, chores, opportunities and challenges staring you in the face. They aren't all equal in importance and you don't feel the same way about all of them. Sort out your to-do's by preparing your LOVE IT, LOSE IT or CHOOSE IT chart. You will need at least one sheet of paper or a spreadsheet program. Create five columns on this chart and at least 20 rows. The first column will contain all the tasks or situations you are currently facing. The second column is "LOVE IT," the third is "LOSE IT," the fourth is "CHOOSE IT" and the fifth is "By When?".

1. Write down all your pending actions in the first column.

2. Decide whether you are going to LOVE IT, which is to fully engage with it, or LOSE IT, which means to either delete it or delegate it, or CHOOSE IT, which will involve shifting your perspective on the task so that you can love it.

3. For now, simply generate the check marks in the appropriate columns. For the LOVE IT or LOSE IT tasks, give yourself a target date for completion. As you can see, the LOVE ITs and LOSE ITs don't present much of a problem. The CHOOSE ITs, on the other hand, are those tasks that are important but that you have trouble getting around to. We will return to the CHOOSE IT column in the "Try It On For Size" at the end of this book.

Sherry decided to tackle her to-do's the LOVE IT, LOSE IT, CHOOSE IT way. The first task that popped into her mind was organizing her home office. Sherry had piles of paper covering most of her desk, and more piles on the floor. The mess was definitely affecting her productivity. She spent time every day going through the piles to find information she needed to do her job; and the clutter was having a negative effect on her attitude about her job. She dreaded going into her office. Getting organized was clearly a priority, but it seemed like a Herculean task. Sherry didn't even know where to begin, and she imagined the project might consume days. Since she did not LOVE IT and couldn't LOSE IT, she put that task in the CHOOSE IT category. While shopping for groceries, Sherry had run into an old classmate, who by chance had news of one of Sherry's long-lost high school friends, Corinne. Sherry was thrilled to find out where Corinne lived and wanted to catch up with her. She put that task on her list as a LOVE IT, and decided to make the call immediately. The holiday season was looming, and Sherry started thinking about the cute holiday hostess apron pattern she had bought a few years earlier. She wanted to embroider one of these aprons for each of the women in her extended family. Each year she felt guilty that she didn't get around to even starting one apron, though she had bought all the materials. When Sherry thought about all she had to do in the next several weeks, she saw that realistically she was not going to find time to make and embroider seven aprons, no matter how thoughtful a gift they would make. She put that job in the LOSE IT column, deliberately deleting it from her agenda, so it wouldn't keep popping up as a nagging obligation.

Pending Action	LOVE IT	LOSE IT	CHOOSE IT	By When?
Organizing my office			X	
Calling a high school buddy I've been out of touch with	X			Immediately
Embroidering seven aprons for gifts		X		

Without making conscious choices about our tasks, they become daunting instead of doable.

GET A NEW HATTITUDE

HATS IN THE WIND TUNNEL

As the LOVE IT, LOSE IT or CHOOSE IT exercise shows, an intellectual understanding of what needs to be done doesn't necessarily lead to a change in behavior. Awareness, though it is required for action, in and of itself is frequently not enough. When knowing isn't enough to catch the wind, it's time to change the direction of the sails, it's time to readjust our orientation. And changing our perspective is something we all have the ability to do, that we instinctively understand and that we have experienced to at least some extent.

When people say something like "I'm going to put on my thinking cap," they are acknowledging that a certain mindset is suited to a particular task. Reading between the lines, people who utter these words are indicating that they are focusing in a way that they don't ordinarily. They are also indicating that they have the ability to bring those perspectives or worldviews to the fore when needed.

This rather primitive mental flexibility is the beginning of wisdom! In truth we have many, many perspectives available to us, many ways to approach challenges and problems, many ways to respond to slights and failures and tragedies, many options for making much of opportunities and successes. When we know in our bones that there is more than one way to skin a cat, we discover we worry less and savor more.

It Happened Just Like Hat

After many years of coaching business and individual clients, Christie Latona and Laura Lind-Blum developed a tool to help people tap into the many perspectives that are available to all of us. The ***One Hat At A Time*®** momentum cards start from the commonplace metaphor of hats to describe the various roles that people play in their lives — parent, manager, volunteer, Sunday painter, choir member, mentor, caregiver, consumer and so forth. Throughout history, hats have been used to identify various trades and occupations, from the sailor's cap to the king's crown to the fireman's helmet. Hats thus provide a rich vocabulary to draw on. The deck contains 27 hat images, and five blank cards, in recognition that anyone who uses the cards will probably want to add to the collection.

The momentum cards are a tool for helping people learn to be emotionally resilient and mentally flexible, and many examples we employ in this book make use of the hats and the mindsets they conjure up. We want to stress, however, that it is not necessary to use the cards to bring the power of metaphor, allegory and analogy into your life. You can start with the vivid images that you or others use to describe situations. You can build on the analogies and images that spring to your mind as you contemplate your own challenges, or hear the voices and witness the body language of people you are trying to help.

The metaphorical approach can be a way to quickly enable people to act on their awareness. Recently, we have been using hat images and metaphors in our work with clients and we've been surprised at how quickly even stubborn, deeply ingrained patterns of behavior can be reversed when people take on a different perspective, by way of putting on a "new hat." Headgear turns out to be a magnificent tool for catching the winds that make change possible.

No, you don't need to go out and buy a miner's helmet or a fortune teller's turban or an artist's beret or an accountant's eyeshade. You already own these hats and dozens more. The hats are metaphors for particular points of view, perspectives, attitudes and competencies.

- A child's beanie, for example, suggests a sense of wonder and openness to experience. It is the attitude of seeing things fresh, as opposed to having been there and done that and knowing all the answers.

- A chef's hat brings to mind the ability to take mundane ingredients and combine and transform them into something wonderful and memorable. It encompasses the idea of using what is at hand, in season and fresh to cook up the best outcome. It may suggest using one's talents to nourish others or to present things attractively to get the best response.

- A cowboy hat calls up an image of rugged independence. It may serve as a reminder to pay close attention to the environment or to rely on inner resources. It may spur you to cut loose from the herd mentality and blaze your own trail.

In the windmill model, **hats are a powerful way of understanding the variety of choices available to us (choose), engaging with whatever choices you have made (be) and creating momentum (do).** Tapping into a wide range of perspectives is like having the 64-color set of crayons instead of the eight-pack. Using the metaphor of hats can enable you to do more and to have more fun and less stress in your life.

It's a Jungle Out There!

Randolph was struggling to make the transition from a forced retirement in a high-visibility career into some kind of meaningful work. He had recently written a book and was asked to speak at a conference for a group of scientists, based on research he had cited and conclusions he had drawn. He felt intimidated at the prospect, and his fear kept him from working on his presentation.

"They're going to eat me alive," he confessed in a telephone coaching session. Using his own image, the coach asked him what it would take to turn those menacing lions and tigers into kittens. Randolph laughed and lightened up a bit at the image of his high-powered audience as a bunch of kittens, but acknowledged that he didn't know what it would take.

*At the coach's suggestion, he spread his **One Hat At A Time** cards out in front of him and looked at them with an eye to finding the card or cards that felt like they would help him discover a way to convert growling predators into cuddly kittens.*

Almost immediately, the coach heard a much more energetic and relaxed voice on the other end of the phone. "The Jester!" Randolph exclaimed. "I don't have to be the expert. I can entertain these people and play a humbler role. I love this!"

Randolph had no trouble metaphorically putting on the Jester's colorful, jingly hat. The image called his inner child out to play. (This is what frequently happens, but if Randolph had talked about the Jester in a matter-of-fact, rational way, his coach would have guided him in a way that would have enabled him to be emotionally and imaginatively engaged, to be able to really wear the hat.)

With the coach, Randolph then explored whether he would need any other hats or attitudes to be successful in his speaking endeavor. He indicated that there was a looming deadline that he was in danger of missing and now he was kicking himself for having procrastinated so long. The coach asked "Do you feel the situation is like a mountain you couldn't possibly climb or that all of the things on your plate are too distracting?" Randoph answered, "No, I'm totally energized about this, and I feel it is possible. I really do get distracted and am afraid that might derail me." So the Miner's hat was called forth for its focusing, illuminative power to get the speech written, slides compiled and deadlines made. Then the Jester went on stage, had those fearsome kings of the scientific jungle eating out of his hand and had a blast!

Randolph's story illustrates the Choose. Be. Do. windmill model. Now put yourself in the coach's seat. In the first part of the dialogue, the objective is to listen for an image or metaphor that encapsulates how Randolph was experiencing his situation. He vividly expressed how he was feeling by conjuring up the image of being eaten alive. If he had not come up with a distinctive image, you might have suggested one or two to him, based on the tone of his voice and what he had to say. For example:

"Sounds like you see these PhDs as a gang of thugs," or

"Maybe you're feeling like you've just been sent to the principal's office," or

"I'm wondering if you see this audience as the Spanish Inquisition all over again," or

"You must feel like these scientists are going to cut your presentation to ribbons."

> "If the winds of fortune are temporarily blowing against you, remember that you can harness them and make them carry you toward your definite purpose, through the use of your imagination."
>
> ~ Napoleon Hill

Once a metaphor has emerged that might be a springboard to understanding and action, you then seek to have them "Choose" a more engaging perspective. In this example, hats were used. Picking a hat or hats to represent a possible aid or solution is usually a quick and intuitive process for people. Randolph immediately gravitated to the Jester. In fact, humor and charm and the Fool's freedom to move around and not be part of any established order were foundational strengths of his, temporarily drowned out by his fear of the scientific bigwigs.

The next critical step is to "Be" that perspective, to engage with it emotionally and imaginatively, to see oneself in that role, demonstrating that attitude and acting out of that mindset. Randolph had decades of experience addressing audiences and giving media interviews. It wasn't stage fright that was afflicting him, but the prospect of being shown up as inadequate in scientific background and knowledge. In a Jester role, he didn't have to have the answers; he could actually ask the provocative questions. He didn't have to defend any conventional wisdom or school of thought; he could be the innocent outsider who noticed that the emperor had no clothes. And Randolph could easily see himself doing those very things.

Once one you get someone envisioning himself or herself in the helpful hat, the "Do" often follows naturally. Having the energy and desire to take action is not a problem. The hat, the chosen perspective, provides the fuel to get the job done. The gap between awareness and action is closed. Sometimes in the doing stage additional perspectives are required to continue the momentum created by the first hat. For example, Randolph needed to wear the Miner's hat to accomplish critical tasks so that the Jester could be successful.

You can use this same process to coach yourself into action.

Before you go to your hat wardrobe, try to identify what has kept you from getting on with the tasks you can't immediately love or lose. Whether it's doubt about your own ability to succeed, the sense that you just don't have the time, crippling anger because you're stuck with the project, or fear of the unknown, you'll probably see yourself in one or more of the thirteen common action blockers in the next section. And, using one or more "hats," you will be able to coach yourself each step of the way to achieving your goal.

WHAT'S BLOCKING THE FLOW?

Resuming our allegory of you as a windmill, there are some things that block access to the wind time and time again. Figuratively, seedlings grow into wind-blocking forests. Developments crop up that sometimes turn a windy tundra into a city with pockets of dead air. At other times, the sail manipulation system or generator needs to be attended to. We find there are thirteen common blockers — or windbreakers — of personal effectiveness and possibility. Which of these is keeping you from doing what you want or need to do?

When You Think You Don't Have What It Takes

Feeling that you're not good enough is often reason enough for not trying to re-position your sails to catch the wind. If we lack confidence in our ability to convert movement into results — why bother?

A focus on weaknesses dogs us through life, from elementary school report cards to annual job performance reviews. Yet trying to fix perceived individual weaknesses is rarely an effective approach to improving either personal or organizational performance. A much better approach is to assume that each person has the attributes he or she needs and to focus on strengths. Organizations need to learn to put people where they can contribute their best and thrive, rather than where they are doomed to fail, or worse, be mediocre. A royal crown is one hat that can help sort out what your "kingdom" is, that set of strengths that truly belong to you, that place from which you can exert real personal power. The chef's hat and the coach's visor are also helpful in identifying your best assets and using them as the starting point for growth and development. This group of hats helps clarify focus and purpose thereby tuning up the generator in the windmill that transforms spinning into something useful.

"Kites rise highest against the wind, not with it."

~ Winston Churchill

When You're Overwhelmed

Ever feel like you are in the midst of a tornado? Working out a merger, putting together appropriate services for an elderly, ailing parent or a learning-disabled child, moving to a new place and a new job — life often throws challenges at us that are so complex we become overwhelmed. We may feel that we're drowning in data and starved for time. We may have the sense that we're doing as much as we can without seeing an end in sight. We may even feel the pressure of the wind so intensely, we may be afraid of breaking a sail or burning out the generator.

Getting through a huge complicated task always requires breaking it down into manageable steps. The miner's lighted helmet and the mountain climber's headgear can help chart a sane, sensible course. They help us shift our focus from the fact that the winds may be too strong into a focus on the simple immediate things we can do to progress.

When You're Convinced It Will Turn Out Badly — As Usual

Some see the glass as half full, and others see it as half empty. The old cliché is true — some people are born optimistic, while others come into the world as little naysayers. It's also true that how we see the world to some extent shapes our experience and works as self-fulfilling prophecy. Optimists are like blondes — they have more fun. And like blondes, some of them were not born that way. Pessimists can learn to be optimists. Instead of generalizing from the unfortunate events and failures that befall them, they can learn to globalize the good stuff and see the occasional bad outcome as the exception to the rule. This is analogous to greasing the sail manipulation mechanism so that there is more fluid motion from one choice to the next and a full range of motion. A pessimistic outlook, on the other hand, severely limits the range of motion.

Coffee Beans Rule!

A daughter complained to her father about her life and how things were so hard for her. She did not know how she was going to make it and wanted to give up. She was tired of fighting and struggling. It seemed as one problem was solved, a new one arose.

Her father, a chef, took her to the kitchen. He filled three pots with water and placed each on a high fire. Soon the pots came to a boil. In one he placed carrots, in the second he placed eggs, and in the last he placed ground coffee beans. He let them sit and boil, without saying a word.

The daughter impatiently waited, wondering what he was doing. In about twenty minutes, he turned off the burners. He fished the carrots out and placed them in a bowl. He pulled the eggs out and placed them in a bowl. Then he ladled the coffee out and placed it in a bowl.

Turning to her he asked, "Darling, what do you see?"

"Carrots, eggs and coffee," she replied.

He brought her closer and asked her to feel the carrots. She did and noted that they were soft. He then asked her to take an egg and break it. After pulling off the shell, she observed the hard-boiled egg. Finally, he asked her to sip the coffee. She smiled as she savored its rich taste.

She humbly asked, "What does it mean Father?"

He explained that each of them had faced the same adversity, boiling water, but each reacted differently. The carrot went in strong, hard and unrelenting. But after being subjected to the boiling water, it softened and became weak. The egg had been fragile. Its thin outer shell had protected its liquid interior. But after sitting through the boiling water, its inside became hardened. The ground coffee beans, however, had a totally different response to adversity. They transformed the water.

"Which are you," he asked his daughter. "When adversity knocks on your door, how do you respond? Are you a carrot, an egg or a coffee bean?"

Optimism is such a superior life strategy that it's worth acquiring and the magician's hat and the halo are the hats that can work the transformation. If you could wave your magic wand, what would you want to appear or disappear? What is the aspect in this situation that you can be grateful for?

When You Just Don't Believe It Can Happen

Our beliefs put the brakes on many things we would like to accomplish. Our beliefs color what we attribute to the wind. How we describe the wind for ourselves, in turn, determines our choice strategy. We may have been told "girls can't do that" (or that trade wind is available to boys only) and grown up sure that was true. You may take as gospel truth that you can't beat the system, or that people don't change, or that you're ugly, or that you don't have much power, or that it's wrong to use power — or all sorts of things. But these are only beliefs, not facts.

The first step to changing self-limiting beliefs is to expose them, and that usually takes some investigative work. The detective's hat is up to the job. Later you may don a mortar board, to help you graduate into a set of beliefs that will better serve your aspirations.

When You're Overcome by Strong Emotions

Grief, anger or both can be so consuming that they keep us from engaging productively with the prevailing winds. Neither endlessly venting and wallowing nor suppressing strong emotion is particularly helpful. What's needed is a means by which we can experience our emotions and yet not be dominated by them, an emotional resilience.

Emotions also influence our ability to choose which way to face the sails. The surgeon's cap is helpful when we need a measure of objectivity to make assessments and decisions, when we must keep a cool head even in the face of raging emotions.

The construction worker's hardhat is also useful for bringing us down to earth and keeping us on course when emotions get out of hand.

When You're Paralyzed by Fear

Fear of failure, fear of success, fear of abandonment, fear of embarrassment, fear of criticism — there's no doubt that fear is a major factor in stalling and remaining stuck. Fear often puts the brakes on the sails, preventing any movement at all. The cure for many fears is just to do the feared thing, while quaking in your boots. And lo and behold, it soon becomes not scary to speak in front of an audience, or to drive in the city, or to dive off the high board.

There are also ways to reduce fear by reinterpreting the rush of adrenaline and the racing pulse as excitement and energy for the doing. Hats that can help contain and transform fear are those of the sky diver, the Viking warrior and the detective.

When You're Burned Out

Sometimes we just feel too drained of energy to do one more thing. The well of ideas and enthusiasm runs dry. It becomes difficult even to imagine feeling excited and motivated to get going. When you're burned out, self-nurturing needs to be the top priority. We might crave a month in Acapulco or a year's sabbatical, but such retreats may not be either feasible or necessary. Life also loses its meaning and zest when too much of what you do is a means to something else, when the course or the volunteer project is undertaken just to pump up your resume, when you go to parties mainly for the purpose of making useful contacts, when you give your spouse a hand with the housework just to score some brownie points.

A way to add energy and zest to life is to do things and enjoy people, just for their own sake, not for what it will get you at some distant date. The beachcomber's visor and

"You must take personal responsibility. You cannot change the circumstances, the seasons, or the wind, but you can change yourself. That is something you have charge of."

~ Jim Rohn

Role Reversal

Dan, a gifted third-grade teacher, encourages his pupils to wear cowboy hats for certain periods of the school day. His young charges imagine themselves riding the range, exploring the unknown, cooking their meals over a campfire, gazing at a vast sky. This powerfully attractive metaphor does wonders to spring the children out of the limits of their role as third grade students. No more do they need to view themselves as relatively powerless, confined, passive members of a herd.

Interestingly, Dan transformed his own role first and was the first to wear a cowboy hat to class. A strong, resilient, self-reliant, adventurous man, he needed to be able to move beyond the stereotype of the elementary schoolteacher and bring more of his own style and flavor to the work.

Metaphor can dramatically enhance our enjoyment of the various roles we all play in life. Wearing your artist's beret when tackling yard work can transform a necessary chore to a thing of beauty. Letting your inner chef lead the meeting can bring out ingredients and produce results that are surprising and pleasing to all concerned. Seeing yourself as a coach can make you into the wise, skilled parent you want to be.

What roles need reversing?
Which ones do you dread?

Jot down all the energy-sapping roles you play and then pair them with new "hattitudes" that would breathe new life into them.

the farmer's old straw hat come in handy for keeping us grounded in the rich, full present moment and for guiding us to small acts and rituals that lead to recovery and refreshment.

When You've Been There, Done That

Much of the time, our experience and expertise work in our favor. They enable us to quickly assess situations and adopt the most appropriate responses and solutions. But at other times, expertise leads straight to ennui. We see a task or assignment coming at us for what seems like the bazillionth time, and actually doing it is too boring to contemplate. It's all too familiar. Or sometimes being an expert in one field makes us blind to other windows on the world. As a journalist, for example, I may have no patience with the detailed, nuanced view of the scholar. As an engineer, I may write off the needs and views of the marketing department.

If you are feeling like the tried-and-true sail position settings aren't being as productive as they could be, it may be time to take a fresh look. Being an old pro tends to shut us off to a lot of possibilities, when opening those possibilities could keep giving us a feeling of freshness in our work. The beanie with the propeller on top is a good one for getting to what the followers of Zen call Beginner's Mind. The fortune teller's turban gets us out of heavily rational, intellectual headspace and puts us in touch with our intuitive knowledge.

When There Isn't Enough Time

Sometimes we feel there are not enough hours in the day to do all we have committed to. Sometimes we feel there is not enough time left in our life to begin something we have always wanted to do, like learning to play the piano, or starting a home business, or building our dream house. Sometimes we feel that the little increment of time that is actually available is not enough to do anything useful with.

It isn't time that we must manage, but our own priorities. With a little detective work, we can usually find out where our time is going and when it is being stolen by activities that are not important to us or not important anymore. And, we can usually recover enough time for things that do matter. The firefighter's red hat can help us distinguish the momentarily urgent from the long-term important.

When Somebody Else Is to Blame

Since we are social beings, almost any challenge that faces us involves other people. Whether we're trying to implement a new customer management system or sell a screenplay, we quickly come up against the fact that some parts of the process are simply not within our control. Fixing the blame instead of fixing the problem can be quite tempting. But to keep engaged with wind, we need to control what we can and let go of the rest. The fisherman's hat gives a helpful perspective here, as do the perspectives gained through captains and cowboys. All of these frameworks speak of resourcefulness, determination, self-reliance and a degree of active patience.

When It's All Work and No Play

Some of us were brought up with a truly oppressive work ethic. We were taught that hard work was the only means to getting anything we wanted or needed. We were raised to believe that work and play don't mix and that play is frivolous and childish. For people with this stern world view, almost anything that comes along – a job, a new assignment, a new house – is perceived as more work. Controlled by the idea of the virtue of hard work, people often find that much of their life feels like a grind.

Fundamentally, we are not machines. Our sails and directional mechanisms and converters aren't mechanical. Our ability to do something playfully versus forcefully versus worriedly versus frantically speaks to our ability to create our own gusts of wind AND maintain the equipment. In

How Do You Row Your Boat?

Row, row, row your boat,
Gently down the stream,
Merrily, Merrily, Merrily, Merrily
Life is but a dream!

Go ahead, sing or read this again. This time, imagine it is an analogy for how we approach life. When asked about which line best captured their week, a coaching group indicated that the first line most resembled them during the week. With lots to do and not enough time to do it all, "rowing" can easily take center stage. It was easy for the group to viscerally understand that without incorporating the other lines of this children's song into their own lives, burn-out and dissatisfaction was inevitable. If you are the boat, the stream is the environment, and the rest is attitude:

What parts of this song do you sing best?

Which lines do need practice?

Are you trying to navigate your boat through rapids or against the stream?

What kind of boat are you in?

What dream are you ready to wake up from?

What dream do you have for life?

Sing this song when you rise and 3-4 times throughout the day as a way to remember and reset your expectations.

fact, the element of play can make almost any task and responsibility sweeter and more life-giving. To turn drudgery into lighthearted doing, the jester's cap, the artist's beret and a party hat all come into play.

When There's Not Enough to Go Around

Just as some people make hard work out of any opportunity, many people (and often the same group) operate from the assumption of scarcity. This keeps them from pursuing many opportunities because they calculate the odds and arrive at the conclusion that they are unlikely to be among the few who will succeed. If one of your underlying beliefs is that there is not enough – money, desirable positions in your company or your field, or ideas for making things better – you are placing unnecessary limits on what directions you will try to tilt the sails. Many hats can help you experience a sense of a wider world and of unlimited abundance, including the astronaut's helmet and the halo.

When It Has to Be Perfect

Imagine that you are responsible for getting the most energy out of a given windmill. Would it be better to stop the sails from spinning until you had calculated the precise coordinates to maximize the available wind or to allow the sails to continue spinning while you experiment with the coordinates? For bringing plans and projects to a grinding halt, few things succeed like perfectionism. If it has to be perfect, it's never finished. If it has to be perfect, we can never take satisfaction in what we have done and move on. If we're going for perfection, we're probably tinkering and tweaking good ideas right out of existence, and missing market windows and other great opportunities.

We can be both more productive and happier when we understand what is good enough. We accomplish more when we commit to approaching life like an experiment instead of like a final exam. The beanie and the astronaut's headgear are useful guides into that mindset.

"Today is life –
the only life you are
sure of. Make the
most of today.
Get interested in
something. Shake
yourself awake.
Develop a hobby.
Let the winds of
enthusiasm sweep
through you. Live
today with gusto."

~ Dale Carnegie

TRY IT ON FOR JIZE

READY, JET, GO!

Go back to the LOVE IT, LOSE IT or CHOOSE IT chart
you began on page (17). For all those items you put in the
CHOOSE IT column, ask yourself:
How can I reframe this task so that it better utilizes my
strengths and makes me feel more excited or energized
about it?

Alternatively, you can use the charts in this section to help
identify the hat, metaphor or perspective that would tilt
the sails in a productive direction. You can use the list of
windbreakers or the emotional signals as a guide.

*An important role Maria had to play as a principle in a
mid-sized consulting company was to make some sales calls
with potential clients. She hated being a salesperson, but
she loved working with clients. She was not able to LOVE
IT or to LOSE IT, so this task fell into her CHOOSE IT
column. After reviewing the windbreakers in light of this
sales task, Maria realized that she felt "She Didn't Have
What It Takes." Following the process of strength-focus-
ing, she realized that she could choose to frame the sales
call as pre-client meetings. Doing so created instant energy and sparks of possibility began to fly!*

ACTION BLOCKER TO ACTION ENABLER CHART

Action Blockers	Action Enablers	Artist	Astronaut	Beanie	Captain	Chef	Climber	Coach	Construction
Belief that I am broken or inadequate / Focus on weaknesses	I'm whole & complete, Have what I need Focus on strengths					X		X	
Sense of helplessness	Own the control that I have. Control what I can and let go of the rest.					X			
Burnout	Recovery and nurturing time								
Why me? Dwelling in the past or the why	What can I do now? Living in the present								
Expert status. (THINKING rules)	Beginner's mind			X			X		
Don't know where to start	Start in the middle (or where I am)					X			X
Grief, anger over lost time or past	Emotional resilience	X	X	X	X	X	X	X	X
Life is work	Can make anything play	X		X		X			
Limiting beliefs	Expose them for what they are					X		X	
Not enough time and/or resources	Spending in line with priorities					X			
Overwhelm	Focus & one small step at a time						X		
Paralyzed by fear	Excitement is flexible		X	X	X		X		X
Perfectionism or need to be right	Good enough Just an experiment	X	X	X				X	
Pessimism	Optimism	X				X		X	
Scarcity mentality	Abundance, freedom, vibrant	X	X	X	X	X	X	X	X

Cowboy	Crown	Detective	Farmer	Financial	Firefighter	Fisher	Fortune Teller	Graduate	Halo	Jester	Magician	Miner	Partier	Police	Sky Diver	Surgeon	Vacationer	Viking
	X								X									
X						X												
			X														X	
			X			X			X			X			X			
			X							X							X	
			X						X						X			
X	X	X	X	X	X	X	X	X	X	X	X	X	X	X	X	X	X	X
X	X				X					X			X					
	X	X					X											
					X				X							X		
												X			X		X	
					X			X	X		X	X		X	X		X	X
X			X			X			X	X	X		X			X		
							X		X								X	
X	X	X	X	X	X	X	X	X	X	X	X	X	X	X	X	X	X	X

CHOOSE A HATTITUDE BASED ON EMOTIONAL INDICATORS

Our emotions serve as our early warning systems; negative emotions are symptoms that we are out of sync with ourselves or our environment. Many speculate that the strong, negative emotions are linked to our fight and flight response to make it easier for us to act and react quickly. And whole schools of thought have sprung up to delve into Emotional Intelligence.

The "Indicator to Hattitude Chart" that follows seeks to make it easier for you to deal with the emotion at hand through reframing the situation so a better choice can be made. Some standard "feeling" indicators are listed in the first column (e.g., complaining, worried, resisting change). Some universally understood hats are represented by 27 columns in the chart. Each of these hats is briefly described in the "Hattitude Snapshot" section.

Start with searching the first column for words that best describe how you are feeling about the situation or task at hand. Once you find a word that resonates, trace your finger across the row and notice which hats might be appropriate for you to try on. Each indicator has an "x" in the columns of the hats that might be appropriate. If there is a hat that is usually a good starting point, a "▲" will appear. If a couple of the indicators fit, you might want to try either looking for the hats those indicators have in common or to figuratively try on the "▲" hats. The "Hattitude Snapshot" section following the chart is designed to help you get into the headspace represented by each of the 27 hats.

Let's say your indicators were "joyless," "insecure" and "complaining." Looking at the chart you find that the "Artist," "Halo" and "Magician" are recommended for all three. So you then go to the "Hattitude Snapshot" pages to look up these hats and let them work their magic.

We encourage you to experiment with using this chart to develop your proficiency in creating hattitudes that allow you to create momentum and results.

If all the x's make you dizzy, you may prefer to do this online at **www.playfulpower.com**. It's free!

INDICATORS TO HATTITUDE CHART

indicators	Artist	Astronaut	Beanie	Captain	Chef	Climber	Coach	Construction	Cowboy	Crown	Detective	Farmer
afraid	X	X		X		X		X	X	X	X	
blaming			X	X	X		X	X	▲	X	X	X
bored	X		X	X	▲			X	X			X
broke		X			X	X		X		X	X	X
burned out	X	X		X	X				X			X
can't say "no"				X				X		X		X
complaining	X		X	X	X			X		X	▲	X
controlling	X		X				X				X	X
crippled by emotions				X		X		X		X	X	X
cut off from intuition	X	X	X		X		X		X			X
cynical	X		X		X		X		X			
denial	X			▲				X		X	X	X
dependent	X	X		X	X			X	X	▲		
depressed		X	X	X	X	X						▲
difficulty with transition	X	X	X		X			X	X	X		X
disappointed		X	X	X	X			X				X
disconnected	X	X	X	X			▲	X	X			X
discouraged	X			X	X	▲	X	X	X			X
distrustful	X	X		X		X	X	X	X		X	X
embarrassed		X	X		X			X				X
empty	▲	X	X				X		X			
exhausted	X				X				X			
failure		X	▲		X	X		X			X	X
frazzled	X				X	X						
insecure	X				X			▲	X	X	X	X
isolated		▲		X			X	X	X			X
joyless	X		X					X				
needy				X	▲			X	X	X	X	X
overly optimistic								X			X	X
pessimistic	X		X	X	X		X		X			
powerless		X	X	X	X	X		X	X	X	X	X
procrastinating	X						X	X				X
resentful			X		X	▲						X
resisting change		X	X		X		X	X	X	X		X
terminally serious	X	X	▲		X							
tense				X					X			X
uninspired	▲		X		X				X			
worried	X	X			X	X		X		X	X	X

Financial	Firefighter	Fisher	Fortune Teller	Graduate	Halo	Jester	Magician	Miner	Partier	Police	Sky Diver	Surgeon	Vacationer	Viking
X	X	X	X		X	X	X	X		X	▲	X		X
X		X	X		X		X		X	X		X	X	X
					X	X	X		X				X	
▲					X					X		X		X
		X	X		X			X	X	X			▲	
X			X		X		X	X		▲		X		X
X	X		X		X	X	X		X	X			X	X
		▲	X		X				X				X	
X	X	X			X			X		X	X	▲	X	X
			▲		X	X	X						X	
		X			▲	X	X	X					X	
X						X	X	X		X		X		X
X			X							X	X			X
		X			X	X			X	X			X	
		X	X	▲	X	X	X	X			X	X	X	X
		X			▲	X							X	
		X			X								X	
		X			X	X			X				X	X
		X	X		X	X			▲			X	X	
					X	▲	X					X		
			X		X				X				X	
					X				X				▲	
			X		X	X								X
	X	X			X			▲					X	X
X				X	X	X	X			X		X	X	
			X		X								X	X
		X			X	X	X		▲				X	
X			X		X		X			X		X	X	X
X							X					▲		
			X		▲	X	X	X				X		X
					X	X				X	X		X	X
	X	X		X				▲	X			X		X
	X	X			X		X			X	X		X	X
		X	X	X	X		▲					X		X
		X			X	X			X			X	X	
					X	X	X		X				▲	
		X	X		X	X	X		X				X	
X	▲	X		X	X		X		X	X	X	X	X	X

HATTITUDE SNAPSHOTS

In both of the charts, we mention specific hats that you might try on under certain circumstances. All of these hats have their own personality and "hattitude." Depending on the situation and your own unique style, the following hattitude snapshots may provide all you need to get started, or just a launching point.

Artist

Creativity abounds!

Put on the artist's black beret and discover that reality really is in the eye of the beholder. Use your imagination to communicate your vision in a way that moves and delights others.

> *What is your inner artist feeling called to create?*
> *What is interesting or beautiful about what you see?*
> *What would it take for you to shift from*
> *imitation to original masterpiece?*

Astronaut

Explore new horizons weightlessly.

Slip on your hi-tech astronaut's helmet and let your smart, curious, futuristic explorer out to play.

> *What new terrain would you like to explore?*
> *What would it feel like if there was no gravity, no heaviness?*
> *What is your oxygen? What is your Source?*

Beanie

Let go of being the expert.

Take the multi-colored beanie out, blow on the propeller and set your inner child free! Feel yourself shift from the rigidity of certainty to the openness of wonderment, of increasing options by decreasing perfectionism.

> *What would make this feel like a game?*
> *What's the WOW factor here?*
> *What if you didn't know?*

Captain

You are the captain of your ship.

Make the wind your ally as you harness it to take you where you want to go. Your inner captain navigates using reliable sources—the compass, experience and the sun. For an experienced captain, uncharted waters are the ultimate thrill.

What adjustments do you need to make now
to best use the available wind?
What is your inner compass saying?

Chef

Transform the mundane into the magnificent!

Let your inner Chef whip up a feast for the senses out of the most ordinary ingredients.

What basic combinations satisfy you?
What feels fresh today?
What can you make with what is at hand?

Rock Climber

Concentrate on finding your next foothold.

Strap on the harness, adjust your helmet and choose which path you are going to take to reach your goal. Your inner climber understands that anything is possible one pull at a time.

What is the simplest way to address the obstacle right in front of you?
What is the next step you can take that will take you closer to the top?
What are you harnessed to in case of an accidental misstep?

Coach

Watch closely and deeply.

Our inner coach reminds us that we can play a role in bringing out the best in everyone we encounter. So – game on!

What is the bigger game here?
What possibilities need to be uplifted and encouraged?
What greatness lies within?

"A man's life of any worth is a continual allegory – and very few eyes can see the mystery of his life – a life like the scriptures– figurative."

~ John Keats

Hard Hat

Get out there!!!

Whether undergoing a do-it-yourself project or a major remodeling, construction sometimes requires demolition. Find your inner carpenter, architect and contractor to get in touch with the importance of structural integrity and joy in translating an idea into reality.

How will you get from the blueprint to the actual building?

What is under construction?

What protection do you really need?

Cowboy

Hit the trails.

Allow your independent, rugged, resourceful adventurer to get the job done. Giddy up!

When you give the reins to your inner cowboy, what happens?

What are you rustling up?

What can you do to simplify the situation so that you can more easily live off of and respect the lay of the land?

Royal Crown

Be in charge.

As the weight of the royal crown touches your head, you realize that claiming your birthright is both precious and a real responsibility. Your inner royal whispers: your ancestors are waiting to be proud of you...

What kingdom are you willing to claim?

Who and what are you responsible for?

What legacy do you want to leave behind?

Detective

Solve the mystery.

Instead of jumping to conclusions, look for clues. Your inner detective will help you piece together the puzzle, question the circumstantial evidence and build the case.

What clues are merely circumstantial?

What and who have you overlooked?

What additional information do you need?

Farmer

Take stock.

Nature has her own cycles and surprises. Your inner farmer is sync with a cycle that is much bigger than your will and desires.

What is it time for?
What isn't ripe yet?
What needs watering and feeding?
What needs pruning?

Financial Advisor

Let the numbers speak.

Slip on the cool eye-shade and notice that green is not a four-letter word. Your inner money maven can help you shift from denial and baggage about money to letting it speak its truth.

If money could talk, what would it say that it needs?
Is your spending and investing aligned with your priorities?

Firefighter

Race to the scene, sirens blaring.

Our inner firefighter is always prepared to respond to a call for help. It knows how to use urgency effectively and quickly distinguishes between life-and-death situations versus false alarms.

What fire needs putting out and which flames need fanning?
What plans and procedures can you put in place
for responding to urgent requests?
Is there an arson or prankster in your midst?

Fisher

Cast your line.

Tap into your inner fisher and experience common sense, patience and calm. You'll find that you'll center action on what you have control over (the location, the lure, the bait, etc.) instead of worrying about all that you don't control.

What are you fishing for?
What lure and casting technique would attract them?
Where is the sport in this?

Fortune Teller

Gaze into your crystal ball and see what emerges.

Let your inner psychic tap into ancient wisdom, patterns and intuition. This isn't about voodoo or new age spirituality. It's about honoring that part of yourself that is in tune with a different frequency than tangible, rational facts provide.

What would happen if I stopped listening to my rational chatter and stepped fully into awareness?
What am I sensing that has no words?

Graduate

Move the tassel!!

The mortar board calls to mind new beginnings, closing chapters or even books, goodbyes and hellos, celebrating accomplishments and moving from one stage to the next.

What are you graduating from?
What are you graduating to?
What ritual can you create to mark the end of this stage?
What's next?

Halo

Step out of the darkness, into the light.

A halo view is a matter of seeing and being in touch with the good and gifts in the present and shifting from a focus on temporary things to eternal/everlasting ones.

What is the gift and good in this moment?
What are you grateful for?
What if this is good enough?

Jester

Ask a silly question.

The Jester's jingly hat lets us tell it like it is — and get away with it. Under the clowning around and absurdity of this colorful character, there's a strong streak of wisdom and common sense.

What foolish question or position will entertain and enlighten?
What kernel of truth does that absurd idea contain?
What can you do to lighten up the situation?

Magician
Abra-cadabra!

Our inner magician reminds us that there is a blurry line between reality and illusion, between how we experience a situation and how others experience it.

If you had a magic wand, what would you make appear or disappear?

What can you transform right now?

What is magical in your own life?

Miner
Focus on what is in front of you.

As the light on the miner's helmet creates needed illumination it simultaneously creates a focal point. Learn what's possible when you shift from a flood light approach to the task or situation to a concentrated beam from a helmet light.

Where are you looking?

What are you illuminating?

What gems are you mining for?

Party Hat
It's party time!

Put on some music, dress up and make it fun! Let your inner birthday boy or girl remind you that most anything can feel like a party.

What can you do to make this feel like a party?

What is there to celebrate?

What if you don't have to make this hard work?

Police Officer
Stop! Police!

Your inner police officer helps clarify and uphold important personal rules and boundaries. Make the shift from catching criminals to upholding the law and notice what changes.

What boundaries need to be maintained?

What needs upholding?

What needs to done in order for you to feel safe?

Sky Diver

Make the leap.

Your inner sky diver is waiting to teach you that fear and excitement are actually the same thing. Preparedness and contingency plans are a waste of time if you don't actually do anything. There is a specific decision point between planning and acting... make the leap.

> *What is your parachute?*
>
> *What are you waiting for?*

Surgeon

Scrub in and get ready to operate.

The ritual enables you to clear your mind of all that might be distracting you from the job at hand. While your inner surgeon cares passionately about creating healing and restoring wellness, he or she doesn't let emotion get in the way.

> *What is healthy, and what needs removing?*
>
> *What emotion is getting in the way of your concentration?*
>
> *What ritual scrubbing in will you do?*

Vacationer

Kick back, relax and restore.

Listen to your inner vacationer and allow it to get you re-grounded, rejuvenated and renewed. Savor what you do, allow yourself to daydream, soak in the possibilities and breathe.

> *What needs renewing?*
>
> *What worries can you release?*
>
> *What can you do to reduce stress right now?*

Viking

Face the issue head on.

Your inner warrior brings courage, honor and strength in even the most hostile of situations. Let it teach you the difference between aggression and courage, between cowardice and fear.

> *What principles must be defended?*
>
> *What cause do you champion?*
>
> *Who and what will you protect?*

NOTE: These snapshots are based on the *One Hat At A Time* momentum cards. For more support for these particular hats, or to buy a deck of your own, please visit: **www.onehatatatime.com**.

THE ANSWER IS BLOWING IN THE WIND

We started by talking about limiting scripts, about how people go through life being "the ugly duckling" or "always a bridesmaid" or "the little engine that could" and never glimpse a way to escape from the box they feel assigned to.

We've found, over and over, that metaphor is the golden escape route, the Yellow Brick Road to the larger life and greater power that really belong to us. Telling what something is like, trying on hats that are new to us, elaborating on the images that pop into our minds are all ways of tapping into more of what is possible.

Through metaphor and allegory, we begin to be able to meaningfully connect our individual selves and circumstances with the larger patterns and forces within which we live. This is what it means to catch the wind, and to actually be the change we want to see in ourselves, our families, our organizations and our world.

Printed in the United States
94661LV00002B/324/A

9 780974 675923